The Six-Figure Quitter

*The Entrepreneur's Guide to Transitioning Out of
Your 9 to 5 Without Regret*

Danielle C. Graves

Legal Disclaimer Notice:

The information contained in this book is provided solely for general informational and educational purposes. The strategies, recommendations, and examples shared reflect the author's personal experiences and opinions and may not be applicable to every individual. This book is not intended to replace or substitute professional advice, including but not limited to legal, financial, tax, or career guidance. Readers are strongly encouraged to seek personalized advice from qualified professionals before making decisions related to their career, business, finances, or personal life.

While every effort has been made to ensure the accuracy and completeness of the information presented, the author and publisher make no representations or warranties, express or implied, regarding the book's content or its application to individual circumstances. The author and publisher disclaim all responsibility for any errors, omissions, inaccuracies, or any other inconsistencies that may be present.

Results achieved from implementing the strategies outlined in this book will vary depending on individual circumstances. The author does not guarantee specific outcomes or results and assumes no liability for any consequences, whether direct or indirect, arising from the use or application of the information provided. Readers are solely responsible for evaluating their personal situation and determining the appropriateness of the strategies described.

This book may include references to third-party products, services, or websites. These references are provided for informational purposes only and do not constitute an endorsement, sponsorship, or guarantee of any kind by the author or publisher. The author and publisher are not responsible for the content, availability, or accuracy of third-party resources.

By reading this book, you acknowledge that you have read and understand this disclaimer. You agree to hold the author and publisher harmless from any claims, liabilities, losses, or damages arising from your use or reliance on the information contained within this book.

To my Starting Five:
God, Mom, Dad, Sister, and Grandma "L"…

Thank you for always holding me down and lifting me up—
even when it didn't make sense.
I'm forever grateful for you.

To Barrhonda…

My first life coach—thank you for holding space for me and
standing in the gap in a season where I was courageous
enough to ask for help.

Table of Contents

1

Intro

" F $&#!" That was the reaction my then supervisor had after realizing the written update I'd just walked into his office and handed him had nothing to do with the multi-million dollar project I was leading. Instead of a project update, this one was personal. The couple of sentences on that paper briefly shed light on my decision to take my talents elsewhere and doubly served as my official two weeks' notice.

His reaction wasn't quite what I expected but, truth be told, I was glad to know that he did, in fact, recognize my impact, after all. At the time, I was serving as project manager for a high-visibility business process reengineering project that would change the way the FBI managed and processed its infamous background investigations. I'd been at the helm of the project since its inception and had the honor of leading a talented group of business analysts and developers. I adored my team and that's what weighed on me the most.

If I can be honest, with each step that I took from my desk toward his office, I was still surprised at the news myself. I'd only made the decision to walk away from my six-figure salary and "good government job"—as they say—less than a week prior without a definitive "plan B" in sight. All I knew was that I was teachable, trainable, and talented, and based on my two degrees and professional experience up until that point, I had options that I was willing to put to the test.

What I would come to discover over the next several years after making that life-changing decision to bet on me and God, is that there comes a time when a high-achieving working professional hits a figurative wall in their career and experiences the phenomenon that I've affectionately dubbed "the mid-career crisis."

It's when you wake up one day and literally ask yourself, "Who am I? "How did I get here?" and "What's the quickest way to exit stage left without turning my life upside down?" Those questions are triggered by what seems like one minuscule grievance. However, when you take an honest assessment of the past few months or even years, you realize that the frustration, career fatigue, and unfulfillment have been mounting for some time, and this is simply the tipping point.

There is a personal threshold for nonsense and organizational politics that we sometimes don't even know we have until the moment that threshold is met. Then, when it finally happens, that's it! You're suddenly awakened to just how uncomfortable you've become in your well-paying career and how it's begun to bleed over into the other parts of your life.

You've obtained all the degrees and done enough moving and shaking to trigger workplace envy from your peers. You've attended all the trainings, obtained the most popular certifications (some that you aren't even using), climbed the ranks, been the consummate go-getter, *and* everyone's favorite go-to. You've managed people, led teams and have yet to meet a problem that you haven't had a hand in solving. You've worked hard and put in enough hours to host your own comp time leave bank. Years have passed you by in the blink of an eye, and while there have likely been challenges and growing pains, the highs of your career—up until now— outweigh the lows.

So, why are you feeling so weighed down? What's missing? Why can't you get your act together and get back to being the dutiful overachiever (and I say that with love) that you've been all these years? What drew you to pick up *this* book?

I'm willing to bet you've reached a point where the hustle and bustle of being on a hamster wheel that's keeping someone else's lights on is no longer satisfying. Actually, that analogy—alone—is enough to make you sit down and reevaluate it all. The things that used to have you jumping out of bed, fully aware of what awaited you in the office, now make you want to turn your alarm all the way off, call out in the name of mental health, roll over, and try again tomorrow.

What's that, you say? Don't get you started about Sundays? Oh, I know all about that, too! You dread them. Because that means Monday is looming, and you'll have to get right back on that hamster wheel to handle someone else's business that's no longer serving you.

But you're tired. Physically, emotionally, mentally and spiritually. Somehow, you've gotten out of alignment, and it's taking every ounce of resilience and tenacity you have to juggle all the balls that adulting and your career have afforded you. I'm willing to bet that's why this book attracted you.

You're looking for permission in one or many of the following ways. Permission to no longer be satisfied with an amazing career and what looks like "having it all" from the outside looking in. Permission to put yourself first. Permission to do the unprecedented. Permission to prioritize joy. Permission to be your own boss. Permission to monetize your gifts. Permission to pursue freedom. Permission to make an impact serving others in an unconventional way. Permission to defy the status quo. Permission for life fulfillment to outweigh a traditional sense of security. Permission to pursue purpose after having spent over a decade (or maybe even decades) developing your expertise and making waves in a field that no longer inspires you quite like it used to. And for the mother of them all—permission to walk away from a six-figure salary while not being one hundred percent certain of what awaits you on the other side of that decision.

Now, let's add a little razzle-dazzle to that, factoring in the time and money (hello, student loans) spent pursuing degrees that positioned you for the success you've amassed to date. Is it too much to ask to love what you do *and* make a living leveraging your God-given gifts? Despite any knee-jerk reservations, there's a part of you that knows it's possible despite lacking clarity on the "how?"

If I can be frank, you want permission to quit what's no longer serving you. Not just *on* purpose but *in* purpose. So, if that's the case, why is it so hard for you to chuck the deuces and move on to more fulfilling pastures? Is it the security of your lucrative salary? Is it the comfort of familiarity? Is it the dangling carrot of a promotion with a more senior title, bigger paycheck, and more benefits? Speaking of benefits, is it the health insurance? Or is it the other perks that come with the job that, while great, are keeping you *cuffed* to a career that's no longer serving you?

"Golden handcuffs" is a name given to those perks and incentives that keep you either willingly or begrudgingly invested. Quite the visual, right? No one in their right mind would just walk away from the safety, comfort, and security of a six-figure salary to pursue unpredictability wrapped in joy and freedom. At least, that's what status quo thinking suggests. But what if you did? What if you faced the ensuing million-dollar questions head-on and actually found the answers?

Where do I start?

What can I possibly do next?

Which of my skills are most marketable?

Which one(s) do I want to use to free myself?

What's my life's purpose?

When is the right time?

Overwhelmed yet? If so–NEWSFLASH–you're smack dab in the middle of your personal mid-career crisis. I know it feels heavy, but don't fret just yet. It's no coincidence that you're reading *this* book at *this* moment. Handing that resignation letter over to my supervisor unlocked so much for me. It opened a world of possibilities I'd never considered. It led me to my purpose and dared me to have the courage to unapologetically align with it. It was also the setup for writing a book–this book–that I didn't even know was in the cards for me. The book that I needed when I was in your exact shoes.

So, here we are. Me, finally being obedient to this particular purpose assignment and sharing with you my blueprint that not only freed *me* from my 9 to 5 without regret but also my clients, year after year. Now, before you roll your sleeves up and dive in, do me a favor and grab a highlighter or a pen.

Got one? Ok, great. I want you to star, asterisk, highlight, and underline this next sentence.

You get to choose.

Because it's true. You do. You get to choose whether you stay or go. You get to choose peace of mind or a toxic work environment. You get to choose fulfillment or unfulfillment. You get to choose strategically exploring possibility or a lifetime of wondering 'what if.' You get to choose YOU over everything else, vying for your time, energy, and expertise.

You. Get. To. Choose.

Like my clients, by the time you finish reading this book, you likely won't hear or read those four words in that order without thinking about me. It's ok, you can thank me later. If what I've shared so far has resonated with you, I want to invite you to keep reading. Take a mini escape from the unfulfillment that has consumed your life and career, and go with me on a journey to unlocking and uncovering what's possible for you. Maybe even finding joy and getting paid for it. If, by chance, you happen to be in a space where you love what you do for a living, but you know there's something bigger and more impactful tugging at you—this is for you, too.

I've taken some time to retrace the steps I took to quit two six-figure careers without regret and create a life I love as a full-time entrepreneur. I call the steps my "7 P's," and I break them down step by step in the pages ahead. I share highs and literal lows as testaments of the journey in hopes that you'll avoid some of the major pitfalls my clients and I have experienced. I look forward to collapsing the time it takes for you to get clear about what's next for you and answering the looming questions of "What's next?" and "How?"

Whether you're beginning to feel antsy in your career and want to be proactive about how you can begin to position yourself for the time, financial, and geographic freedom that your heart desires, or, if you're already beyond frustrated at this point and desperate for an exit strategy that affords you peace of mind—read this from cover to cover *before* you quit. Consider yourself warned that once you see what I'm getting ready to share with you, you won't be able to unsee it.

My only asks of you while reading this are that you: (1) remain open to the possibilities that may present themselves seemingly out of the blue, (2) take the suggested actions that I recommend, in order, and (3) don't expect to be the same person by the time you finish. We have some strategizing to do and a pair of golden handcuffs to unlock, so let's get to it. The *key* and freedom you've been praying for are very likely much closer than they appear.

2

Unorthodox Beginnings

I've found that there are patterns to your life's purpose. If you take a moment to reflect on everything you've experienced throughout the course of your life up until now, there are more clues in that, alone, than you might imagine. The ebbs, the flows, the heartbreaks, the losses, the breaking points, and the defining moments are all pieces to the bigger puzzle of why you are here on this Earth. It took me a while to realize it, but hey, you know what they say about hindsight.

I was born into a military family stationed in South Carolina in the early 80s. By the time I turned two, I'd already had one move under my belt. This move took us to Hampton, Virginia, which became the place that I would ultimately call "home." Fresh out of pre-school, my parents enrolled me in Hampton University's Laboratory School, which was the on-campus elementary school. I entered first grade with my six-year-old peers, and halfway through the year, my teachers called my mom and dad in for a meeting. The teachers informed them that while I was indeed excelling, I wasn't being challenged by the work. So, my teachers proposed moving me to the second grade for the remainder of the year. My parents agreed, and as a result, I completed two grades in one school year. Skipping a grade is one of the earliest pieces of my personal "puzzle" that I can remember.

I'm pretty sure my parents didn't see that curveball coming, but nevertheless, they opted to lean into the opportunity that presented itself and made a decision that would forever change the trajectory of my life. It was a decision that would impact who my K-12 classroom peers would be over the years and set me up to graduate from high school at the age of 16. It impacted the scholarships I'd qualify for when I enrolled in college and where I'd be when I first got the dreadful news on 9/11. It adjusted the timeline on when I'd graduate from college and that it would end up being before I turned 21. It played a role in when I graduated from grad school and the internship opportunities I'd qualify for. It also factored into me being in the right place at the right time to be selected into the first class of FBI Staff Operations Specialists in the fall of 2007.

I don't know if they realize how much of a role they've played in all of the seemingly independent, moving and shaking I've done over the years, but they were, in fact, the catalysts of it all. All because of *one* decision to position me to be challenged instead of allowing me to settle.

They got to choose.

And choose they did. They chose calculated risk. They chose opportunity. They chose not to let me settle or play small. They chose possibility. They chose challenge on my behalf, ultimately giving the green light for me to be "skipped." Most of all, they chose to defy norms.

When I look back over my life, I can see clearly now that I've been on an unintentional fast track from the beginning. It took me about three decades to slow down enough to catch on to what God had seamlessly planned for my life. Every room I've been in, I was supposed to be there. Every obstacle I've faced was meant to prepare me for what's to come. Every person whose path crossed with mine has been divine, from those who have blessed my soul to those who have agitated me all the way to my next level.

Now, imagine that same little six-year-old girl being uprooted from the comfort zone of her first-grade classroom with her friends and escorted down the hall to a new class with new peers who were already familiar with each other. That was one of the first times my inner introvert experienced having to embrace the discomfort of leaving the familiar to pursue greener pastures filled with new beginnings and many unknowns.

After that unique combined year of first and second grade, I went on to spend another school year at the Lab School before transitioning into public school for fourth grade. Another change. Another new environment. New people. New surroundings. More new beginnings. Then came the military transfer orders back to South Carolina. That meant a new state, a new school for fifth grade, more new surroundings, and *more* new beginnings.

"Uncle Sam" would dictate another transfer just a year after that, that would have us to move again—*back* to Hampton. I ended up going to four middle schools over a three-year period and finally put down roots for my high school years. I rocked my green and gold and was proud to be a Bethel Bruin. I roamed the same halls as NBA Hall of Famer Allen Iverson not long after he was there, and, fun fact, even made the JV and Varsity basketball teams.

After all the moving and adjusting I'd done the eight years prior to high school, having a chance to matriculate from freshman to senior year under the same roof with my peers and chosen friend group was priceless. What I had no way of realizing then, during some of those uncomfortable times of being uprooted, was that I was building muscle. Mental muscle. Adaptability muscle. Not being afraid to do things even if it meant having to do them by myself—muscle. Making friends in new places muscle. Ambivert muscle. Leadership muscle. Move to the beat of my own drum muscle. Courage muscle. There are too many more to name, but I think you get where I'm going.

Over a decade later, as a gainfully employed adult, when it came time to make unpopular decisions that most people didn't understand or even agree with–that muscle memory kicked in. When opportunity knocked, I was open to embracing the discomfort of "new" and the unknown to take on internships and full-time employment in the bustling big city of Washington, D.C., as a twenty-something. What a time to be alive and legal!

When life handed me lemons, I wasn't afraid to call off an engagement—less than a month out from the planned wedding date and $8,000 down the drain. I, instead, proceeded to make strawberry lemonade while adjusting and adapting to an alternative storyline for my life that I'd never considered. When I wanted to travel on a whim and experience the world, I'd do my research, book the trip, let my parents and sister know, and go. Even if it meant traveling internationally by myself and, unintentionally, stressing my mother and grandmother out. When my six-figure career became unfulfilling, I refused to settle. I, instead, explored possibility, calculated the risk, created opportunities when they didn't seem to exist, and bet on God and me. Twice. Just like my parents did when they made the decision to skip me to second grade.

I'm now wise and self-aware enough to know that it was all a part of the plan. A plan that would set *me*, quite the unassuming underdog, on a path to blaze trails wherever I showed up in the world without even trying. A plan that, quiet as kept, would foster inclusion in the storied FBI through a different lens—my lens—making it more equitable and desirable for marginalized leaders and generations to come. A plan for me to support, motivate, inspire, lead, and empower the next generation of game changers—including *you*.

All that I've seen, experienced, and overcome up until now has influenced my passion for unapologetically living a life I love, even if I have to do the unprecedented to create it for myself. Throughout the next few chapters, I will walk you through my blueprint, outlining the exact steps I took to pivot out of two six-figure jobs that were no longer serving me and into the life of my wildest dreams. I'll refer to each of those pivotal moments of my life, respectively, as Leap 1 and Leap 2, as there are nuggets that I've drawn from each experience that I'll be sharing with you. My invitation to you is to keep an open mind and be sure not to count yourself out before you've given yourself a fair shot at what, right now, may seem impossible.

3

Power to the Pause

I know you're ready to hit the ground running so you can tap into your purpose and exit stage left sooner than later, but first, I need you to *pause*. Even if the adrenaline is pumping, you're excited about reading this book, gung-ho about figuring out what's next, and beyond ready to map out your exit strategy. Your professional expertise, analytical mind, and ability to solve problems that appear complicated to most people will serve you well on this journey to pivoting out of your 9 to 5 without regret. However, the first step to freeing yourself from those golden cuffs and allowing you to unapologetically throw away the key has nothing to do with any of that.

Before you take another figurative step, I literally want you to *pause*. Stick with me. We're going somewhere. There's not only power *in* the pause, *but* there are levels to it. What do I mean by *pause*? I mean, slow down. Change up your routine. Take some time for self-care. Do something or some things that will help you disengage from the main sources of your frustration and unfulfillment.

When was the last time you detached? By detach, I mean letting go of worry, control, angst, and the posture of hyper-focus on what doesn't yet exist. One of my favorite ways to detach is to get distracted, and my number one recommendation is to do that via intentional activities that bring you joy. It's easy to distract yourself with other woes and worries that come with adulting, leadership, business, and entrepreneurship, but you want to be intentional about doing the exact opposite.

One of my favorite questions to ask my coaching clients is, "What do you do for fun?" Over the years, I've observed a common theme in their responses. It's something they have to really sit with and explore because they spend so much time serving others at home, at work, and in their community. They've managed to prioritize everything else while juggling more balls than they can count on autopilot and, somehow, make it look easy. The list includes but is not limited to parenthood, the 9 to 5, significant others, caregiving, church, sorority/fraternity, managing a home, other important relationships, and the side hustle that they would love to be the main hustle.

So, where does that leave the things that make their heart sing? On the backburner and still on their "bucket list!" I, personally, don't believe in bucket lists because of the grave nature associated with them. I've made it my business to turn the notion on its head and take the things that would have been on such a list and make them a priority–NOW.

Why wait to do the things your heart desires? Who said you had to? Why can't you do them now? What's in the way? What are you waiting for? What permission do you need to give yourself? How gratifying might that be for you to begin checking off boxes much sooner than later?

In case you've been able to escape it thus far, burnout is real. It's even more egregious for high achievers because we are wired in a way that affords us the capacity to do many things well, but at an expense if our time, energy, and joy are not properly managed. Yes, joy needs to be managed just like time and energy, and I'll scream it from the mountaintop. WHAT ABOUT JOY?!

One evening, during my daily two-hour commute home from Washington D.C. to Richmond, Virginia, I said something out of seemingly nowhere that, to this day, still surprises me. "My life is out of control. I think I need a life coach." I wasn't enjoying life or the fruits of my literal labor, and I knew I was too young for that to be my plight. Steady on the hamster wheel in the name of money. Not feeling in control of my life but, instead, controlled by it. Enough was enough. I had to get back to me. I had to prioritize the things that made me happy. I had to do what can sometimes be hard for us go-getters. I had to start saying "no."

"No" opened up time for me to sit on my couch and aimlessly catch up on my favorite shows that I rarely had the time or energy to finish. "No" came in the form of using my paid leave for sanity's sake and not just the next exotic vacation. In fact, I leveraged it to carve out time to do whatever my heart pleased.

"No" looked like me being intentional about the hours I worked, with the goal being to get in and get out. Nothing more, nothing less. "No" meant disappointing loved ones who were accustomed to my presence and dependability. Saying "no" outwardly meant saying "yes" to me in so many more ways that I'd previously taken for granted.

It gave me time and space to just *be*–whenever I wanted and wherever I wanted. I was able to quiet the noise of other people's needs and opinions, *pause*, and hear myself think. And it felt good. That series of "No's" was the precursor to Leap 2, but for Leap 1, my *pause* looked very different.

It was a milestone birthday year for me, my sister, and one of our favorite cousins. We were turning 30, 25, and 30, respectively, so I came up with the bright idea for us to take a trip. We started planning months in advance and our travels landed us in St. John, U.S. Virgin Islands, smack dab in the middle of their annual Carnival celebration and the 4th of July. We couldn't have planned it better. It was a dream vacation filled with sensory overload, warm hospitality, beautiful beaches, a luxurious villa, a private boat excursion over to the British Virgin Islands, delectable food, and beautiful culture.

It was just the break I needed from the rat race and frustration with my job. As much as I loved my team and the responsibility of leading a group of talented and dedicated go-getters, the politics had begun to get the best of me. Not seeing eye-to-eye with my leadership didn't help either. If you've had the honor of serving in a leadership capacity, then you know that being the buffer between your team and your management can weigh on you.

St. John was the pattern interrupt that I'd desperately been needing, and it did my mind and body good. I went back to work the Monday following our trip–which I've since learned never to do after a vacation–and shortly after getting settled, I was welcomed back to the tune of a microaggression in my first meeting of the day. I made a mental note of it but blew it off in that moment. Just like that, I was back at it on the hamster wheel, and the afterglow of my vacation was gone.

At the time, I was living in Baltimore, Maryland, and commuting to work in Washington, D.C. I would drive about 15 minutes to catch the commuter train, ride about 45 minutes into D.C., and then make the 20-minute walk or take some form of mass transit to my building. It was quite the commute but normal for an average commuter in the DC-Maryland-Northern Virginia (DMV) area. On my second day back from my vacation, I decided to take the bus for the last leg of my commute and believe it or not, I was already exhausted all over again and wishing I was back on the island.

I grabbed my preferred window seat on the bus, and as I settled in, I remembered the meeting from the day before. The microaggression resurfaced, and it got me thinking. There had been mounting discontent between me and the "aggressor" prior to vacation, so this snub didn't come as a surprise. But this time, something about me was different. I felt different. I felt lighter. I *was* different. Not having to be "on guard" while being whisked through the city on the bus at that moment afforded me the opportunity to allow my mind to wander without disruption. Even if it was only for a few short city blocks.

I remember asking myself, "Why am I putting up with any of this?" I took a quick assessment of my life and honestly pondered why I was allowing myself to settle for any of the nonsense like I didn't have options. Those golden cuffs will have you in the Twilight Zone if you're not careful, and at that moment, I was in the process of snapping out of it. The reality of the matter is that while I was making six-figures and living a comfortable lifestyle—whenever I actually took the time to enjoy it—my job needed me more than I needed it.

I had no debt. I was living with my grandparents to save money to buy a home, so I wasn't tied to a lease of any kind. My car was paid for, so there was no car note, and by God's grace, I didn't have any student loans. Yet, I was in the matrix and so disconnected from my truth. Pulling back the layers and getting completely honest with myself, I recognized that I was the prize. I threw humility out of the window for once and sat in that. I no longer loved what I was doing. I simply loved the people that I got to serve, lead, and work alongside, in addition to the wins we accomplished as a team.

I knew that my team would run through a wall for me. And I'm certain they knew that if duty called for running through a wall, they'd be running through it *with* me. Looking out the bus window, passing city block after city block, I affirmed that I was skilled, teachable, trainable, and dual-degreed. I had options that I simply had not opened myself to exploring while being that hamster on a wheel, keeping everyone else's lights on.

There were times when I'd made attempts at updating my resume but found myself waking up the next morning with the laptop in my lap and my resume *still* incomplete. The job and the commute were taxing, and the little energy I had at the end of the day wasn't enough to set me up with the solid exit strategy that I wanted and desperately needed. When I realized the job was in the way, I decided—at *that* moment on *that* bus—that I'd had enough, and my savings could buy me some time to recharge and reset.

Traffic that morning on the bus, coupled with the onboarding and offboarding of passengers, bought me just enough time to call a few people on my Personal Board of Directors and simply ask for support in my decision before getting off at my stop. Not financial support but moral. The knee-jerk responses from everyone I reached were balanced. Some said yes with no hesitation, and others offered a voice of reason to reconsider because, you know, I had a "good government job."

Truth be told, my mind was already made up, and no matter what, I was giving my notice. The only question was—when? Talk about the power of the pause. My vacation unlocked the clarity and confidence that I'd been missing. I had everything I needed all along, but thanks to the foggy haze of burnout, I just couldn't see it.

Years later, after both leaps, I was working with a coaching client. Let's call her Sharon. During her 90-day coaching engagement with me, she decided she was ready to give her notice and take the leap. Before our paths crossed, pursuing full-time entrepreneurship was something she'd wanted to do but didn't quite have the confidence to do. However, after a couple of sessions, she made the executive decision to give her notice and pursue her wildest dream of being her own boss.

She got to choose, and *choose,* she did. Knowing what was waiting for her on the other side of her decision, I encouraged her to both celebrate and take some time off to reset (i.e., *pause*) before she hit the ground running full-time in her new venture. Not only do I recommend pausing at the outset, for clarity's sake, but I highly recommend you pause before jumping into the next thing.

Sometime later, we connected, and she mentioned wishing she'd taken heed of my suggestion back then. She'd been going nonstop juggling the responsibilities of adulting and full-time entrepreneurship and was now feeling the imbalance of it all. I believe in the pause. Let me say it again. I BELIEVE IN THE PAUSE! Taking the time to prioritize joy, detach, and use a different part of your brain is a much-needed pattern interrupt when preparing to transition out of your 9 to 5.

A pattern interrupt is one of the most underrated life hacks. Especially when clarity is not so clear, and your mind is cluttered with all things life, work, leadership, and business. The routine that you've strategically curated to ensure you manage and handle it all can actually do you a disservice in times like this because you're running on autopilot. You have to break that up. Do something or some *things* to evoke different emotions.

Your pause can look however you'd like. The only requirements are that it prioritizes joy, temporarily takes you away from your normal routine, and distracts you from the never-ending barrage of questions running through your mind about what's next. My all-time favorite go-to is traveling. Hopping on a plane and escaping to a destination where the water is blue-green, and the drinks are pretty and sweet. I'll even get behind my camera, put on my photographer hat, tap into my first love, and literally freeze time. I'm also notorious for curling up right at home with a good romance novel and getting lost in the story. If you've never read a Beverly Jenkins novel, you're missing out. *Your* healthy escape, on the other hand, could look completely different. Life may not allow you to whisk yourself away right now and that's okay. You might have to get creative.

The goal is that you intentionally remove yourself from your typical routine and get comfortable saying "no" to the status quo. Change your scenery, mood, and mode to do whatever brings you joy and allows you to focus on something other than the "problem" at hand. For clarity's sake, I call it The Perfect Pattern Interrupt.

Here are a few ideas for The Perfect Pattern Interrupt:

- Take leave/PTO in the middle of the week.

- Plan a staycation at a local hotel.

- Tap into your inner artist and book that class that you've been wanting to take.

- Go to the theater and watch back-to-back movies.

- Take a scenic drive or plan a road trip.

- Take a train ride (day trip or overnight).

- Book that candle-pouring class.

- Start that crafting project.

- Take a whole week off from work and spend the time unapologetically doing whatever you want—even if it's absolutely nothing.

- Binge-watch that show (or three) that's been on your list for months.

- Put that long overdue date with your friends on the calendar *and* see it through.

- Move that bucket list item that you've earmarked for retirement to the top of your list and do it now!

Are your wheels spinning now? If you do any of the above, partake at your own risk. No matter what you choose, even if it's something not listed, get creative and do what works for you. My sole recommendation is that you make sure you check these boxes:

- Change your scenery.

- Do something that requires you to be present in the moment and focus on the task or activity at hand, and temporarily forget about your life and career woes.

- Make sure that whatever you do brings you joy.

- Don't think about work or what's waiting for you when you get back.

- Email me what you're committing to do for your pause (yes, I'm for real–dg@daniellethecoach.com).

Clarity breeds confidence, and I attribute the clarity I had that morning on the bus to my *pause*. If you haven't taken time off, please grab your phone right now, check your calendar, and pick a day or seven to get away and immerse yourself in things that bring you joy. And don't be shy about using your leave. If you need a mental health day, sick leave will do if annual leave won't. Your mind is part of your body, and if your mind is not well, it's imperative that you use the resources you have readily available to help you strategically navigate what's next with a sound mind.

Also, don't cheat. Your *pause* isn't to work on your exit strategy. Your *pause* is strictly intended for you to clear your mind and reset so that when the time comes, you can look at your life and what's possible for it through a much clearer lens. I know it might feel hard to do, but no cheating! You deserve this.

4

In Purpose

Since my initial pivot from public service into full-time serial entrepreneurship, it's been important to me to ground myself in why I'm doing any of this in the first place. Hindsight being "20/20," it's clearer than ever that the very thing that keeps me grounded these days also served as the *key* that unlocked possibility for me during my mid-career crisis.

Why am I here? How did I get here? How can I turn my life right side up without dismantling or disrupting my most meaningful tethers?

Those are just a few of what felt like millions of questions that ran rampant through my mind as I was trying my best not to succumb to a life of zombie commuting and a career that was draining the life out of me. It seemed as if one question spawned 17 more and took me deeper into the trenches of "what ifs" and "if-thens" until one day, a three-word question bubbled up to the surface and forever changed the trajectory of my life.

What's my purpose?

It was the come-to-Jesus moment of all come-to-Jesus moments. Why hadn't I thought about my purpose or at least considered it before then? Of all the self-help and personal development I'd done up until that point, I was never once led to consider the reason for my existence in the first place. *"Why am I here?"* came close, but there was something about *"What's my purpose?"* that stirred my soul.

After that aha moment, none of the other questions mattered to me. I knew that whatever I did next had to align with my purpose so that I wouldn't start something new only to end up feeling just as unfulfilled and discontented a short time later. Whatever came next career-wise, I wanted to love and make an impact for the greater good. The million-dollar question then became, *"Well, what's possible?"*

I eventually came to realize that, contrary to popular belief, plenty is possible *in* purpose. There's a misconception that purpose is one-dimensional, and whatever yours is, you're stuck in that box for life. Is that not the most drab, solitary confinement-sounding scenario ever? I'm happy to tell you that aligning with your purpose is nowhere near as bleak as that may sound or as limiting as you may have believed. Purpose is freeing, joyful, impactful, grounding, and, though not exempt from challenges and complexities, it offers a sense of ease and flow that's often missing when you're misaligned.

I bring this up right here and right now because no matter where you are on your entrepreneurship journey, there's no time like the present to factor *purpose* into your equation. Especially after a *pause*. It served me at the very beginning of figuring out what skills and gifts I would capitalize on in a business of my own. It continues to serve me now when the woes of entrepreneurship have me questioning, *"Why am I here?"* and *"How did I even get here?"* Sound familiar?

I wish I knew where I came across this information back then because I absolutely want to credit the source. However, I am unsure where I first saw, read, or heard this particular concept on how to find my purpose. I take no credit for it, but I will share the rabbit hole I journeyed down to uncover mine.

A quick internet search on "How do I find my purpose?" will present tons of resources with plenty of them being Venn diagrams. The premise that I explored is that your purpose can be found at the intersection of at least three things:

1. What brings you joy?
2. What are your God-given gifts?

3. What do you do that serves others?

While you reflect on that, grab a pen and notepad and create a three-column list with one column for each purpose point. Label the first column 'Joy,' the second column 'Gifts,' and the third column 'Help.' This isn't a one-and-done exercise, so let me manage your expectations from the start. It takes time. That is, time for you to embrace the art of *noticing*, which is having the presence of mind to observe what's happening in and around you, in the moment, while it's happening.

I believe with my whole heart that your answers to these questions have been hiding in plain sight right in front of you all along, but because you haven't been looking for them in this way, you simply haven't noticed. If you took the last chapter seriously and accepted my invitation to pause, then you should have a fresh take on what brings you joy. More specifically, the activities, people, and experiences that light your soul up from the inside out. What are they, and who are they? List them, without judgment, under the *Joy* column. What do you do with ease that most other people don't or can't? What is that thing, or what are those things? List them, without judgment, under the *Gifts* column. What do people tend to come to you for help with? When I say "people," I mean anyone who contacts you and asks you for help. From the simple tasks to the large asks. Consider friends, parents, children, siblings, colleagues, supervisors, associates, members of organizations in which you are affiliated, and even strangers. List those asks, without judgment, under the *Help* column.

Write down what immediately comes to mind in this first sitting without judgment, and also plan to add to each list as you begin *noticing* over time. Notice how you show up in the world. Notice how you respond to people and situations. Notice how others respond to you. Notice what lights you up. Notice what irritates you. I can't stress enough the importance of moving through this exercise without judgment. I know how high achievers are wired, often discounting the "little" things we do, which are, sometimes, the answers we've been searching high and low for. There are no wrong answers. So, if you dismissed a knee-jerk thought from your list, go back and add it while it's top of mind. Everything is fair game. Let me tell you how I know.

Leap 2 came on the heels of me accepting a new position and realizing less than 30 days into it that it wasn't a good fit. However, one of the blessings that the position afforded me was meeting and getting to know new people. Sometimes, it was putting a name and personality to a face that I'd seen in passing for years. Other times, it would be meeting people that I never even knew existed.

When I first joined this particular team, a colleague in a sister unit stopped by our space and noticed that I was new. Let's call her Colleague A. She was kind and inquisitive. Before I knew it, she was sharing her side of an unfavorable work situation she'd been navigating which I wouldn't have been trusting enough to share with someone I'd known for less than an hour. I listened and validated her sentiments on the matter, and then I went back to work. She would have never known this on her own, but I'm naturally a vault, so her business was safe with me. Over the next several months, we'd see each other in passing and exchange pleasantries. Occasionally, I'd be given unsolicited updates on the situation she shared with me during our first exchange. This was purpose clue number one.

In an unrelated encounter, after I'd officially begun trying to uncover my purpose, I found myself assigned to another special project. This time, I was on the receiving end of a vent session with one of my new project members, who was also new to my network. Let's call her Colleague B. Once again, I was made privy to personal and work-related situations that I was quite surprised were being shared with me—especially since we were barely workplace acquaintances. It was that second conversation that was the 'aha' moment for me. My *noticing* hinted that there was something about me that made practical strangers comfortable sharing their personal business with me. Although they weren't outright asking me for help with something, they were silently asking me to *listen* and, at times, soliciting my opinion and advice.

I thought about my life outside of those two conversations. It became clear as day that I was a confidante for many of my friends, family, and even former colleagues with whom I had longstanding relationships with. People came to me for me to listen and to offer solicited advice. *I was on to something.* Then came the epiphany about how much I enjoyed encouraging and motivating other people to advocate for themselves and live their best lives. That was the icing on the cake.

Looking back, I always had an inner desire to pursue a career in therapy or counseling. Turns out my desire was in alignment all along even though I ultimately went a slightly different route with coaching. Unbeknownst to me, my *gift* of active listening was always there, flying under the radar and serving me and others. Every single day. Doesn't everybody listen? No. They absolutely do not. Not selflessly. Not intently. Not actively. Not the way I do. That revelation was a defining moment for me and is a major reason why I'll forever unapologetically spread the gospel of *purpose* because it's both powerful and empowering.

Another key to gaining awareness about your purpose is to pay attention to patterns around the situations and circumstances you've overcome. Case in point, do you remember the broken engagement that I mentioned? Believe it or not, that experience gave me the courage to later take Leap 1, in faith, and walk away from a job that was no longer serving me. Five years after that, I took Leap 2 with even more faith. Now, here I am, a decade after Leap 1, writing a book to share with you how I did it, lessons learned, what's waiting for you on the other side of your leap, and why considering your purpose is so important.

I can see clearly now that I'm built to take calculated risks, blaze trails, defy the status quo, and empower others to take calculated risks of their own. Honestly, I don't like talking about the broken engagement. I made a decision that I am forever proud of and that's that. But, never in a million years did I expect the outpouring from other women across generations about how my decision deeply affected them. They've privately shared how they felt encouraged and redeemed through me because, at some point in time, they'd chosen to settle for less than they deserved.

Although it was a pain in my behind at the time, that situation was so much bigger than me. I know that I didn't go through that just for myself. I went through that for a multitude of reasons and people. Since accepting that fact, I'm a lot happier to reshare my annual Facebook post to my timeline when it pops up in my memories section. The post is a love note from the "seasoned" me to that version of me who decided to choose faith over a faux fairytale. It celebrates the anniversary of me making that courageous decision, and like clockwork, the post garners new comments, fresh reactions, and private messages, sharing just how timely my post was to another courageous soul.

Purpose isn't always pretty, but somebody has to stand in the gap. At the end of the day, when the dust settles, and it's just me and my thoughts about who I am, why I'm here, and how on earth I'll be able to keep going, the common denominator is *purpose*. This whole new career and life that I've co-created with God has all been because of *purpose*. When it hits you, "everything" seems to all of a sudden make sense, and hindsight comes into play again. While the semblance of understanding, in the moment, is extremely gratifying, deep down inside, you know that grasping a full understanding of the bigger picture can be forever fleeting. It's simply par for the course.

If you're on my email list and you've ever read one of my Danielle The Coach® emails, there's a 100% chance that my signature reads…

In Purpose,

Danielle

This work that I do is not just *on* purpose, from coaching to speaking to writing this book and everything else that's in store. It's all rooted *in* purpose. As you populate your three columns and add to them over time, begin looking for opportunities that can be derived from marrying at least one element from each list. What opportunities are intricately situated at the intersection of what you love to do, what brings you joy, and what serves others?

The answer to that question may not jump out at you the first time or three, but keep exploring. Don't let up. It's a process that can take some time. Don't be afraid to think outside the box and create an opportunity. You may find at least one— but hopefully several—avenue(s) of possibility that can free you from your career as you know it without regret. You get to love what you were purposed to do. That does not mean you will always enjoy every moment of your purpose-aligned journey. However, it does mean that it makes it less arduous than exerting effort and energy in spaces and places that are not in your immediate zone of gifting.

Here's my elevated take on purpose. I believe that our lives have an overarching purpose that is directly related to the God-given gifts that we are born with. Throughout different seasons of our lives, we have different purpose assignments that align with our overarching purpose. For many who have not reached this point of purpose-*full* enlightenment, there is zero awareness of their purpose at play. They simply exist and figure out this thing called life the best way they know how. Riding the rollercoaster, holding on for dear life, and going with the flow. This is not a bad thing. It is what it is. However, what tends to happen is when they find themselves in a pinch and begin feeling the squeeze in their personal life or career, they misconstrue the root cause of their discontent and unfulfillment.

When one purpose assignment ends, another one awaits you. Staying in a place, space, or posture beyond the fulfillment of your purpose assignment is a breeding ground for complacency, contentment, unfulfillment, and discomfort.

All of these symptoms can be present at the onset of a mid-career crisis. Maybe you're uncomfortable because there is more for you to do elsewhere. Maybe your purpose assignment has been fulfilled, and your spirit, gifts, know-how, and expertise are needed in another arena or in a different capacity. Just maybe you're being awakened to the bigger calling over your life, and you're being presented with the choice to either play small and settle for the status quo or trust your gut and make a move by faith. Every assignment has a beginning and an end, and if we're not careful, we can linger in a place or frame of mind that has, pun intended, served its purpose.

The early years of my career were like something out of a storybook, especially for a young Black woman in the FBI. For context, the largest and most dominant demographic group was White male special agents, a generation or two my senior. I was being tapped for special project after special project, jet-setting all over the country on the government's dime. I was engaging with some of the highest ranks of the organization, expanding my professional network far beyond my wildest dreams, and being promoted up the ladder pretty quickly. Interestingly enough, I began to notice that my experience seemed like an anomaly for other young professionals in the organization. Primarily those who looked like me.

It bothered me for several years in a way that nagged at my conscience and constantly tugged at my heartstrings. Until one day, I had the epiphany that when something bothers you, there's a good chance you're supposed to do something about it.

Purpose.

So, ok. That was confirmation, but what in the world would *I* do about it? Not long after my epiphany, I'd had enough. This was a few years after Leap 1, and I couldn't take it anymore. It was like an itch that I absolutely had to scratch, or else I was going to lose it. The hard part for me was figuring out who I wanted to help most. Millennials? Or African-American millennials?

After giving it some thought and consideration, both had my heart. However, I decided to engage the group that was most underrepresented in the organization. African-American millennials. My initial goal was to connect my friends in the building and share resources that I'd gleaned from all my moving and shaking. I felt there was no reason any of us should find ourselves across the table from one another in the boardroom—if there so happened to be two of us in the room at the same time—and not have any knowledge or familiarity of one another.

I'm sure you know well that business transactions can go a lot smoother when there's an existing relationship or common denominator. So, if nothing else, I wanted to do my part to bridge that gap. I gauged the interest of coworkers from different teams, experiences, and projects I'd been on with whom I'd become friends. One hundred percent of the responses were in the affirmative, so I planned an informal gathering over lunch. About nine or ten of us gathered at a round table. New introductions were made amongst perfect strangers, and, for others, it was an opportunity to put a face with a name. My network was meshing well like I'd envisioned it would.

The information and resources I shared were tips about the most random topics ranging from personal finances to navigating the organization. It was a literal brain dump of all the things I'd been holding over the years that I just wished other people knew. It was such a relief to have gotten that off my chest. The feedback from the lunchtime gathering was overwhelmingly positive and there was a consensus to meet monthly and for everyone to tell a friend and bring a friend.

In two years' time, that informal roundtable of 10 of my colleagues-turned-friends quickly morphed into what is now known as FBI African American Millennials (FAAM)— pronounced 'fam'—a grassroots employee resource group (ERG). In that same time span, FAAM amassed a listserv of upwards of 300 employees from all across the organization of different ages, races, and ranks. All by word of mouth. No marketing campaigns. No formal backing. Just relationships, networking, and the perks of offering a solution to a problem that otherwise would have gone unsolved.

It went from being an informal networking circle to a monthly meeting focused on leadership development, mentorship, and how to navigate the organization. By this time in my career, I was pretty well connected, so I began calling on my own mentors and seasoned connections to join us and share their leadership journey and lessons learned. The across-the-aisle dialogue that this sparked was a game-changer.

The kicker was when my mentors and contacts would come to one of our lunch meetings to speak to the group and leave just as inspired as the millennials in the room by the rich conversation that wasn't being had in most spaces. That led to not only FAAM regulars telling a friend and bringing a friend but also my mentors and non-millennial colleagues spreading the word and recommending each other as good people to be in the room.

Within a year or so of FAAM's formation, this type of grassroots organic buzz led us to an intimate roundtable discussion with the number three in command of the FBI, at that time, to simply talk about leadership development. What was powerful and unforgettable about that day was that there was no pomp and circumstance. No special assistants in tow. No "new faces" that wanted to impress the "boss." It was just us.

He came by himself to the small conference room that we'd reserved and pulled up a seat. Not at the head—but smack dab in the middle of the table. The minority in a room filled with young, eager, melanated faces. We had a direct but casual conversation about his journey climbing the ranks, what it was like to navigate the organization from our vantage points, and respectfully candid dialogue on culturally relevant concerns surrounding relations between people of color and law enforcement.

This type of engagement was completely unheard of. Little did any of us know, there was so much more to come. Overnight, FAAM became a "household" name. Before we knew it, there was a waitlist of senior executives and staff who wanted an opportunity to get in front of the group and share their wisdom. One of our invited speakers even joked about telling the then-Director of the FBI that he was unavailable because he had to go speak to FAAM. Yes, that really happened, and if you know anything about the chain of command in a paramilitary organization, that spoke volumes. It was a moment that will forever be etched in my heart.

Never in a million years did I intend or envision that lunchtime meeting of the minds with friends that January afternoon would morph into what FAAM had become. A respected, self-led ERG of millennial African-American leaders who were making waves changing the culture of a century-old organization—together.

FAAM provided a platform for the otherwise overlooked. It put a battery in the backs of some who were counting their days until they bid the Bureau adieu. Instead, it inspired them to change their vantage point and be the change they wanted to see by pursuing and leaning into leadership opportunities. I've lost count of the stories I've heard of FAAM members pursuing and being tapped for opportunities that they otherwise wouldn't have even considered. Imagine being a Black law enforcement officer or employee during the social unrest that occurred in 2020 when George Floyd was publicly lynched by Minneapolis police officers. FAAM was what the Bureau didn't even know it needed, and its mark on the FBI will be etched in the archives.

Purpose.

Starting that group was my assignment. The FBI had been around for almost 110 years at that time. Yet, it wasn't until *I* got there that a movement of the sort had been initiated. What started out as taking inspired action out of frustration turned out to be *in purpose*. I wasn't looking for it. I simply answered the call that came from within. Now, imagine if I'd never acted on it. I, honestly, can't.

The countless hours I've spent pondering, noticing, and identifying patterns in my life have paid off. My purpose is to SMILE. Literally and figuratively. My smile is often complimented, and I'm forever grateful to my parents for investing in great dental and orthodontic care during my formative years. On the figurative side, looking through my purpose frame, I am certain that I've been put on this earth to *Support*, *Motivate*, *Inspire*, *Lead*, and *Empower* the next generation of game changers. See what I did there?

I know why I'm here and what I'm here to do. I have evidence of the power of my purpose and my alignment with it. I'm clear on my why, and I dare anyone get in the way of what I was put on this Earth to do. My purpose is bigger than me, and yours is bigger than you. Just like me, you were created for a time such as this. So, what are you here to do?

5

Plan

Gaining clarity around your purpose gives you options, and as with everything else, *you get to choose.* You get to choose *when* you show up, *where* you show up, and *how* you show up. In doing so, you make conscious decisions that are either in alignment with your purpose or not. It's just that simple. Your purpose is your *why.* The *what* (you're going to do next) is your strategy that will free you from your 9 to 5. The *when, where,* and *how*—combined—make up your plan. Whatever you do, devise a plan. If you can help it, don't quit without one. It can be detailed or loose but have one. Your confidence and ability to quit without regret are rooted in a plan that you believe in. It doesn't mean that implementing the plan will be easy, but you will, at least, have clarity about where you're going *and* some semblance of how you're going to get there.

Taking a calculated approach to deciding how you want to make your leap positions you to create and choose an exit strategy that aligns with your lifestyle. It allows you to factor in both your personal obligations and the pace at which you want to make your pivot. Know that your strategy may require asking for help, and have no shame in enlisting or investing in the support and accountability you need.

The calculated approach is ideal when you have the time, space, and grace to figure things out with minimum pressure. That's the semi-perfect scenario. However, I know firsthand that, sometimes, there isn't time for a grand exit strategy that's been curated and allows for flawless execution. Sometimes, for the sake of your mental health, there isn't time for one because you need to make a move *now*.

When I briefly contemplated Leap 1, my strategy was cut and dry. I was going to make my grand exit and take intentional time to rest, reflect, and regroup to gain the clarity I needed about what was next. That meant leaving without another job lined up but with complete faith that I'd have options when I was ready and opportunities at the right time. Besides, I had a good seven years of professional experience working for the esteemed FBI by that time.

There was a spectrum. On one end, I knew I could leverage my math degree to get into teaching. On the other end, there was a world of open-ended possibilities in the realm of tech that I couldn't even wrap my mind around. Regardless, I knew there was hope on the other side of those four walls. I also knew I'd be ok even if it meant sacrificing my six-figure salary and taking a pay cut.

In that season of my life, it was as simple as that for me. To be completely transparent, I could afford that simplicity. I was unmarried with no kids, no major obligations, no debt, and enough savings to last me several months. I had the upper hand, and I played it to my full advantage. That type of fluidity may not work for you if your lifestyle isn't as independent or flexible as mine was at that time. You may have dependents, student loans, and major bills to consider. Or your risk tolerance may not be that high. And that's ok. The ultimate goal is to figure out what works for *you* so you can create an exit strategy and plan that aligns with your lifestyle.

For Leap 1, my strategy was to go back to school to do, in this life, what I always joked about doing in my next life. I was going to get a Ph.D. in Psychology. My subsequent plan to make it happen was fairly simple. Find a program, apply, get accepted, and then make my move. Or so I thought. Though the vision was clear, I was so mentally and spiritually taxed that I only had enough energy to devise a loose plan to support the strategy and trust that I'd bring it to life once I officially freed myself from my 9 to 5.

Although I'd done the preliminary research, I acknowledged that days were passing, and I hadn't applied to a single graduate program. I'd been running on fumes, on the brink of burnout, and doing my best to simply exist. Acknowledging how taxed I was, I decided that the clarity I had around my exit strategy and loose plan alone was enough for me to confidently pull the plug and submit my resignation. I trusted myself to put the plan in motion once I freed up some mental space and was on the other side of my decision.

At the outset of Leap 2, I had no earthly idea what I wanted to do next. Things were different this time around because there was more at stake financially. I had a mortgage, and I refused to settle for just another job. I didn't have the luxury of leaning on a loose plan like I'd done five years prior. I needed something that excited me. Something that made an impact. And something that allowed me to leverage the many skills and gifts I already possessed.

I never in a thousand years thought that taking Leap 2 would land me on a local news station at the height of The Great Resignation in 2022, sharing tips to consider before quitting your job. But, as destiny would have it, there I was, standing on set in the NBC12 studio, under bright lights and with cameras all around. I thought it was worth a shot to pitch the segment, given the mass exodus of career professionals from the workplace becoming a growing trend and topic of conversation. It also helped that March 31st, aka "International Quit Your Crappy Job Day," was on the horizon. Yes, there really is a day for everything, and I was right about my timing. The network accepted my pitch, and after tracing my steps that led to Leap 2, I was able to share with their audience a snippet of what I'll share with you here as you think through your exit strategy.

First things first. Let's talk about the elephant in the room. Finances. Money talks, and we all know it. I first learned about the term "F-U Money" before taking Leap 1. It tickled me to my core when I first heard it because it painted quite a vivid picture but also spoke volumes about the necessity of saving and having sound finances to prevent you from feeling held hostage to a job or career.

What's your financial runway? How long can you sustain your lifestyle without bringing in another dollar? How much do you need to pay your bills and survive? There's a difference between what you *need* and what you *desire*. Especially if you currently have disposable income. *What's your number?*

The goal is simply to get you in the space of realistically understanding what you minimally need in order to live, while the ultimate goal is to unlock your earning and wealth potential via entrepreneurship. It's a great idea to enlist the help and guidance of a financial or wealth advisor to help you think circumspectly about what's next, what's possible, and how to maximize your financial resources.

My clients are typically making upwards of six-figures or more when they find me. They are ready to make the investment to gain clarity about what's next and are also in a prime position to invest in any additional support they may need. Full-time entrepreneurship is as rewarding as it is challenging. The more you plan your finances on the front end, the more thankful, prepared, and confident you'll be as you embark on your entrepreneurial journey.

Now, let's talk about paid time off. If you're anything like I was when I was on my corporate grind, you may have a substantial leave bank at your disposal. I can't stress this enough. USE YOUR LEAVE. Factor it into your plan. Sick leave. Annual leave. Paid time off. Whatever you call it, use it. If your mental health is being impacted, recognize that sick leave is your friend. Take the time you need to reset so that you can put your best foot forward and be in the best position to play the long game.

Don't sleep on your annual leave or paid time off, either. It's easy to think about saving it for a vacation, but it can come in handy to spend time doing absolutely nothing, for once, or checking off tasks on your never-ending to-do list. You know, adulting. You can also use the time to make progress in your side hustle, which will soon be the main hustle. There's something powerful that happens when you have time to be still, unplug, and let your mind wander. You know that, though, because we talked all about it back in Chapter Three. So, go ahead and take a moment to look at your calendar and decide when you're taking planned time off in the near future. Embracing the *pause* is a lifestyle, so let's keep a great thing going.

Now, here's something that you may not have considered planning for. Not everyone will support the decisions you are preparing to make or understand why you would ever want to leave the "security" of a well-paying job or a salary that some can only dream of. Support and accountability are one thing. Non-judgmental support and accountability are a whole different ball game. So, if you're serious and want the latter, hire a life coach. I say it not only because I am one but also because I am able to write this book and share my story because of the impact of hiring one myself.

Something in me knew that I needed accountability to get out of the space of feeling stuck and unfulfilled with my life and career. I knew it was up to me to do something about it, and I had to be honest with myself about my mounting fatigue. If I wanted to see a change sooner than later, I needed help.

My network proved itself reliable, and a good friend offered a recommendation for a life coach whom they knew. I reached out, and we had a successful chemistry call that ended with a date on the calendar for our first official session. Problem-solving is something I'm naturally wired to do, so although there was some time between my chemistry call with my coach and our first session, my brain was still in fix-it mode. By the time we had our first meeting, I was even clearer about what I wanted to do next, but my dilemma was seeing it through in spite of the burnout.

My exit strategy for Leap 2 was to pivot into the field of professional coaching. I knew without a shadow of a doubt that I wanted to be a life coach. I knew that I could wake up the next day and declare that I was a coach, and it would be so, given the non-regulated nature of the industry. But, in true high-achiever fashion, that wasn't enough for me. I wanted to step into the marketplace with credibility. I was aware that it would be a process of finding my certification program of choice, enrolling, and fulfilling the requirements before becoming "official," and I was game for it. That was the beginning of my plan.

When I first connected with my coach, I requested her help with keeping me accountable so that I could pivot seamlessly and in the shortest amount of time possible. Left to my own devices, I knew it would be easy for me to allow fatigue to win night after night. What I didn't want to do was wake up months or a year later and find myself in the same place. So, instead, I set myself up for success and invested in the help I so desperately needed. I tell prospective clients all the time that no one wants to come to a session with their coach not having done what they committed to doing in between sessions. That baked-in accountability is a difference maker even for the most seasoned go-getter.

So, what do you want next? What direction are you pivoting into? Which gift or skill are you planning to monetize in alignment with your purpose? What's your strategy? What's your plan?

Remember, your strategy is the *what,* and your plan is the *how.* See it. Write it down. Put it in motion and take it one step at a time. Before you know it, you'll look up and find yourself living in what was once just a dream. Ask me how I know.

6

Put People on Notice

Once you get clear on your purpose, and you've figured out what you can leverage from your know-how in combination with what it is that you love, then it's time to *put people on notice*. Whether you realize it or not, and whether you like it or not, as a seasoned professional or even part-time entrepreneur, you have a reputation. You're known for something. Whether it's a certain skill, set of skills, or particular characteristics, your reputation precedes you. When a certain problem, need, or topic is raised, you are top of mind for someone. If the themes that cause you to come to others' minds don't align with the new direction that you're pivoting into, then there's some additional work for you to do while you're putting your plan in motion.

For me, what I was known for was two-fold. Professionally, I was known for leading people and projects, being well-connected, having an enviable work ethic, being a trailblazer, founding FAAM, and being a dependable "rockstar" employee who had executives vying for my talent and insights.

On the personal front, something that I undoubtedly was known for was photography. Most people connected to me had no idea that I even worked for the FBI until I posted about it on my last day. To this day, past photography clients and people in my network still reach out for photo shoots, and I absolutely still oblige them. It's a blessing to be the go-to person for a service or skill that serves others. Yet, it's important to remember that you have a say in changing the narrative when it's time for you to be seen in a different light.

Once I decided that becoming a coach was my next move, I acknowledged early on that I needed to reprogram how my network viewed me. So, I did what any wise person on the brink of a life transformation would do. I rebranded myself. No one in my immediate sphere of influence was talking about coaching, nor did anybody view me as a coach, so I needed to change that.

My strategy was to leverage social media to begin planting seeds and inviting my connections on the journey with me. Up until then, I'd been able to get away with being a consumer of information on my social apps of choice with the occasional photography post or advertisement. But now,

I had to become a content creator and begin marketing myself in a way that I'd never done before. It required a level of transparency and vulnerability that was normally reserved for my inner circle. It also required me to agitate my inner introvert and lean into the uncomfortable space of sharing my energy and *business* with the world. I'm proud to say that I both shared *and* lived to tell about it.

It started with a post sharing that I'd just submitted my application for Georgetown's Executive Certificate in Leadership Coaching program. It took every ounce of energy and brainpower that I had left after commuting, working, and adulting day in and day out. But, with the unwavering support of my life coach, I got it done, and I asked my social media "friends" to whisper a prayer on my behalf.

Then, about six months later, I shared again when I learned that I'd been waitlisted for the program. I was excited and hopeful because that was better than an outright rejection. Not long after that, I shared the news that I'd been waiting for. I got in! Not only did I get in, but I was also invited to join the very next cohort and wouldn't have to prolong putting the next part of my plan in motion. My social media family celebrated right along with me.

I went on to share a picture of my "first day of school," and every month, when I'd report for my weeklong training, I'd share a snapshot or two of my experience. About a month and a half into the program, I parted ways with the FBI after twelve years of public service, and, yep, I shared that, too. For many people, it was their first time learning that I worked there in the first place, and for some, it was a surprise to hear that I was moving on. My social media feeds were becoming more interesting, and the engagement grew with each post.

I not only pulled back the curtain of my super private life but also focused on creating videos related to personal development and mindset. I shifted from a content consumer getting lost in the never-ending social media scroll to a strategic content creator. It seems like it happened overnight, but the reality is that "overnight" was really a combination of time and consistency over the course of at least a year.

That was all a part of the plan for Leap 2 when it came to putting people on notice, but not so much for Leap 1. For Leap 1, I wanted to play my cards right and leverage my annual leave, of which I had plenty before I officially separated. Being politically savvy, I wanted to be sure of my rights to use my paid time off prior to offboarding. So, before submitting my leave request for my supervisor's approval, I went to HR late one afternoon to ask around.

It was late enough that most of the early risers were already gone for the day, but, to my luck, I found someone still at their desk who could likely assist me. Growing up, my mom always said, "Nothing beats a failure but a try," so I politely interrupted the HR Specialist and asked my questions. She followed up by asking a couple of probing questions to help her better assist me.

Once she got the gist of what was happening in my world and that I was getting my ducks in a row, she asked if I could come back the next day and speak to one of her colleagues. I'll never forget it. She asked me to come by early that next morning, which was no problem because I normally arrived pretty early anyway. So, when I got in and settled the next morning, I made my way back up to her desk.

She walked me over to her colleague, who must've been expecting me because when she saw us coming, she hopped up and said, "Let's go in the conference room." We made our way to a vacant conference room, and I thought it was a bit odd when one of them closed the door behind us. I was on a mission to get the answer that I was looking for, so I didn't pay too much attention to it.

Once we were seated, the newest addition to the party asked, "So what's going on? We know that you've done a lot in the organization. Most people this young in their career don't have the experience you've had to date. So, what's up? Why are you leaving? It'd be a shame for the organization to lose you." Now, at this point, I'm feeling a mix of irritation and gratitude. The irritation was because I'd made up my mind and wanted a simple policy-informed answer. However, the gratitude quickly outweighed it. Before I realized it, the conversation shifted from an HR consultation to an honest, transparent exchange that felt like a kitchen-table conversation between a niece and her aunties who don't play about her. If there were sleeves to roll up, theirs were, and they were ready to fight the good fight to talk me off the ledge and get me to stay.

They tried their best to get me to change my mind because "I had so much going for me." But what they didn't understand was the mental gymnastics that had gotten me to that point in the first place. My mind was made up, I knew my value, and I also knew what was possible outside of those "four walls." I was done, and that's exactly what I told them.

I'd already put my leadership chain on notice that I was leaving, and now, after speaking with these two ladies, I'd unintentionally put a few more people on notice, too. I'm not even sure if I got the answer to my original question about my annual leave. However, based on what transpired after I left that conference room, I'd say that I got way more than I bargained for.

After my impromptu conference room cornering, I went on about my day. I returned to my desk a few hours later after another meeting and was greeted with an unexpected voicemail. It was from a former supervisor that I had a lot of respect for and had thoroughly enjoyed working with. She relayed that she heard I was leaving the organization and wasn't quite sure what was going on, but if there was any interest in staying, she was growing her unit and had an opportunity in her space. She also knew of an executive who was looking for talent to staff and support the organization's growing Diversity and Inclusion office.

Word sure has a way of traveling fast, and she had me at Diversity and Inclusion. I couldn't believe it. When I woke up that morning, I had no idea how quickly putting my plan in motion *and* putting people on notice would move the needle for me. The way doors of opportunity opened for me was nothing short of a miracle that met me on the other side of my faith. My gut had told me to go up to HR and advocate for myself that random afternoon. What I didn't know was that acting on that hunch would serve as the catalyst to a breakthrough that was beyond my wildest dreams.

To this day, I call those two ladies my HR angels. Sometimes, I fight back tears when I think about how selfless and persistent they were in advocating for me. They swooped in, inserted themselves in my situation, gave unsolicited advice as only an auntie figure could, and went out on a limb to call in reinforcements. All because I *put people on notice*.

Similarly, that's exactly what I encouraged one of my clients to do, too. My client is a talented, educated, driven leader with decades of experience on her resume leading people and change. Accolades aside, she'd found herself in a position that you and I know all too well, either from firsthand experience or from the anecdotes of other go-getters in our spheres. She'd been fighting to exist in a toxic environment while having her leadership undermined. By the time she enlisted my support, she was just about at her wit's end. The microaggressions and years of feeling unable to show up as her most authentic self without posing a threat to others' insecurities had her feeling jaded and unfulfilled. She'd made attempts at applying for new jobs, and though she would see glimmers of possibility in the application process, they all fell flat.

Her investment in coaching was not only an investment in the support and accountability that she needed. Her investment energetically put every vice and adversary on notice that she was coming for everything that was hers. While her qualifications and resume alone spoke for themselves, she was not leveraging all of the tools in her toolkit. With over two decades of experience, she not only knew a lot and had seen a lot but also managed to do a great job connecting with others. She had a network that, for some reason, she was not leveraging. When it came to putting people in her network on notice, there was nothing but untapped potential.

She took heed of my recommendation, leveraged LinkedIn strategically, and informed industry peers and former colleagues about her interests and openness to taking on new challenges. Interestingly enough, a former colleague just so happened to know of an opportunity that fit the bill of the type of leadership role that she was seeking. And guess what? She was the right fit, in the right place at the right time, and she got the job and a pay bump!

Your ego will have you working harder and not smarter. It will keep you feeling safe and frustrated simultaneously and will keep you stuck in places that are no longer serving you. Let this be the last day it delays your breakthrough.

Who do you know that may have answers or insights that are relevant to your plan? Who do you know that is already taking up space in the figurative arena that you are moving into? Who absolutely needs to know that you are planning to take the leap? Who has come to mind recently that you've yet to reach out to? Now that you have clarity on the new direction that you're going in *and* what you want to be known for, you have the luxury of controlling the narrative and letting it be known what you're up to next.

Begin to establish yourself in the world from *that* vantage point and start telling people who you are. Reframe and recreate the lens that people see you through. I'm sure I could have taken both leaps and lived to tell about them without enlisting the support, wisdom, guidance, and accountability of others. What I'm unsure of is how long it would have taken me to find myself and my footing on the other side of each leap had I not shared my plans with a select few.

If you've read this far, I think it's safe to say we probably have a few things in common. You're likely built a little different from the majority in that you aren't comfortable settling for the status quo, and you also aren't afraid to think and dream big. You likely have no desire to hear the opinions of naysayers who couldn't fathom leaving what, on the outside looking in, seems secure. Not even if you have to endure daily toxicity coupled with unnecessary roughness just to do your job.

For that primary reason, amongst others, I understand the hesitancy to share that you're entertaining the thought of pivoting out of your safe, secure, and well-paid career. You don't want to hear the judgment and opinions of people who simply don't get it or would never understand how you could consider betting on yourself. If I'm on your pew, I want you to know that your feelings are valid and you are not crazy. However, I encourage you to open up to the idea of strategically putting people on notice. Be open to possibility but also prepared for radio silence. It can go either way.

As always, *you get to choose* when and how you go about it. I just need you to recognize the power of leveraging your network and taking control of the narrative as you rebrand. You never know when you may be entertaining angels. Or better yet, when angels may be entertaining you.

$\underline{7}$

Posture

When I first started making noise online about how I help entrepreneurs who are still juggling a 9 to 5 with creating their corporate exit strategy, I began receiving invitations to share my insights on other creators' platforms. I'll never forget one host, in particular, asking, "How do you know when it's time to quit?" Before I could even think about it, I replied, "When your faith outweighs your fear." It's so easy to say and even simpler to grasp conceptually. However, flexing your faith muscle in real life, in real time, in the face of opposition and other people's limiting beliefs, can be way easier said than done. It's all about your *posture*.

Who in their right mind would consciously walk away from the familiarity and relative security of a six-figure salary? I'll tell you who would have the audacity to do such a thing. Someone who understands that there is a purpose in all things. Someone who understands the importance of aligning their time and talent with the very reason they were put on this Earth in the first place. Someone who understands that they are on assignment and are being called to make more of an impact by doing something different. Someone who recognizes that there is more to life than their comfort zone. Someone who understands both the importance of exercising loyalty to oneself and the consequences of self-betrayal. Someone who is beyond tired of feeling stuck on start. Someone who has been reminded of just how powerful they really are, especially when they're operating in their zone of genius. Someone who is no longer looking or waiting for someone else to save them. Someone who is willing to unapologetically make a short-term sacrifice for a long-term gain. Someone who is resourceful and willing to tap into their network. Someone who refuses to settle for *"What if?"*

That's the type of person who would have the gumption to bet on themselves and God. Even when, to the status quo-conditioned eye, it makes absolutely no sense. One day, you have every reason why you shouldn't leap. Then, after doing the work of getting clear on who you are in this season, where you're going, and how you're going to get there (i.e., your plan)—the game changes. You put one foot in front of the other and do what you have to do in order to free yourself from what's no longer serving you. And dare anyone to get in your way.

I often tout that, after working with me, the people in my client's lives have three options. They can get on board. They can get out of the way. Or they *will* get bulldozed. I say that because my clients are going places—with or without them. And so are you.

There's a certain swagger that you have to have about your decision to pursue possibility. While I was counting down to Leap 1, I ran into a friend one afternoon in the hallway at work. By this time, I'd given my inner circle at the office a heads-up that I was leaving, so she knew that my time was winding down. My friend asked if I was scared because I was walking away from a six-figure GS-14 salary. Without hesitation and with a sincere smile, I said, "Nope. I'll be fine. I have options." And I meant it with every fiber in my body. My certainty didn't come from having my next gig lined up because, at that time, I had nothing in place. Nevertheless, something in me knew that I would be ok.

Sometimes, people are sent to test us. Instead of holding true to what we know in our gut, we allow their insecurity, uncertainty, or genuine curiosity to distract us from our assignment. But what happens when we stand firm in our faith, no matter how crazy the "call" may look or sound? I am here to tell you that unwavering faith is the catalyst to freedom. Just days after that hallway encounter with my friend, my HR angels kickstarted the series of events that I told you about in the last chapter. I got recruited back before officially separating, without a break in pay or service. The rest is history. I didn't see that coming, and I'm confident that it was nobody but God. I am one thousand percent confident that the surety I had in response to my friend's genuine and understandable curiosity unlocked something for me that day.

Faith moves mountains. Faith opens doors. Faith ushers in possibility. Faith releases control. And faith births other believers when you put people on notice. Those on my Personal Board of Directors who weren't so sold on me taking Leap 1 also grew in their faith. They could not believe the series of events that unfolded right before all of our eyes, but after sitting with the miracle that was my truth, they ultimately had to.

When the Great Resignation first became a hot topic, I had almost three years under my belt as a full-time entrepreneur after taking Leap 2. The corporate world seemed to, all of a sudden, be experiencing a mass exodus of talent at alarming rates. Around this same time, I was part of a business development community where my peers were other entrepreneurs. Some were full-time in their business, like me, and others were juggling both the 9 to 5 and their business on the side.

One day, one of the members, let's call her Tracy, announced that she was planning to submit her resignation letter on March 31st–International Quit Your Crappy Job Day. As the self-proclaimed Quit Queen, I messaged her, congratulated her on her decision, and offered my support if she ever needed it. Besides, I learned about the holiday from her, and she was the inspiration behind my pitch to my local news station. She took me up on my offer, and we hopped on a call. Her power posture was locked and loaded. She knew that she was pulling the plug on her three-decades-long career, and she was also crystal clear about what she was going to do next. So, as an expert at chucking the deuces and living to tell about it, my primary advice for her was centered around what to anticipate once she submitted her resignation letter.

Some think the hard part is giving the notice. I'd argue that the plot thickens when you're on the receiving end of a barrage of questions, opinions, and judgment. If you stay ready, you don't have to get ready. I want you to be prepared just like Tracy was. Here are three things I recommend thinking through:

1. **Be prepared to answer the "Where are you headed next?" question.**

You can answer it however you'd like but just be prepared to answer it. Want to keep it vague? Sure. Do that. But, again, I stress, have an answer ready. Once word got out about Leap 1, I was ready to let it be known that I was going back to school to pursue a Ph.D. That's it. For Leap 2, I cared a little less, and when asked, I would share that I was starting my own coaching practice. One of my favorite recommendations on how to answer that question is, "I'm taking a sabbatical." Remember, you get to control the narrative, and the best way to do that is to plan for it.

2. **Be prepared for your leadership to roll out the red carpet.**

They may ask if there's anything they can do to get you to stay or even postpone your departure. If there's something that you want, know what it is *before* you hand over your resignation letter. Tracy took heed to my advice and negotiated to stay onboard for an extra month but with two weeks' vacation built into that time frame. Imagine that!

What's the worst that can happen at this point? They can say no. And guess what? That's okay because you were prepared to peace out without any extra frills anyway. I urge you to do your due diligence in the event that your employer becomes generous and willing to accommodate you and your needs. Be sure to weigh the pros and cons of whatever perks may be on the table and exercise political savvy while asking for what you need. If you find that there isn't anything that can be offered to appease you or support your exit plan, that's ok, too. *You get to choose.* Just make sure you think it through.

3. Contrary to #2, be prepared for your leadership to watch you walk right on out that door.

If you're as valuable to your organization as I believe you are, I'd be inclined to think that your leadership would feel an immediate loss with the mere mention of you leaving. Whether they do or not, I want to be as honest with you as I was with Tracy and make sure that you are as prepared as possible.

I, personally, have experienced both. In one instance, there were talks about how they could get me to stay. In the other instance, they sent me on my merry way and held the door open for me to walk right on out. I was one hundred percent ok with that because I wasn't calling anybody's bluff. I was going to be ok, regardless. I knew it. I meant it. I stood firm in it. I believed it with every fiber in me. And, ultimately, I was.

Your *posture* matters. Physically, mentally, emotionally, and spiritually. What thoughts are you thinking about your leap? What's your emotional state when those thoughts bubble up? What's your body language saying that maybe your mouth isn't? How much do you really believe in your vision and your plan to bring it to life? Does your faith outweigh your fear? What areas need some work?

If there's at least one area that you've identified, don't judge yourself negatively and please don't beat yourself up. You deserve grace, and if it comes from anyone, it should most certainly come from you. You've put people on notice, and they're not going to just stare off into space. They're going to do what people do best. They're going to inquire about where you're going next. Some will do it out of sincere interest or concern, and some will undoubtedly inquire just to be nosy.

Whatever you do, make sure your *posture* on the matter exudes confidence even if you don't have all the answers right now. If you catch yourself "slouching," make the adjustments and put your game face back on. Find and sustain a posture of expectation that it's coming. That it's going to work. That it's going to take off because you're putting yourself in position and doing the work to accomplish and receive the very things that your heart desires. Your *posture* is a catalyst for the peace, clients, revenue, abundance, freedom, and fulfillment that your soul is longing for. Your *posture* positions you for your *next*.

8

Prove It

Now that you have clarity about your purpose, a solid plan, and the confidence to put it in motion, do you have everything it takes to make the leap? You very likely do. Do I recommend leaping now? I don't. Not yet anyway. Not without some social proof. Proof that there's a desire or need in the marketplace for what you plan to sell or offer. Proof that who you plan to sell your product or service to even wants it in the first place. Proof that your target audience is willing to buy it at the price point that you want to offer. Proof that you can sustain yourself for however long you need to once you remove the security net currently known as your 9 to 5.

There are levels to quitting without regret. There's the level of unquestionable belief in what you're planning to pivot into next. Then, there's the level of establishing proof. This is not to discount your inner knowing and the work you've done up until now to firm up your faith muscle. Having proof simply validates the direction that you intend to go in fulfilling the vision.

If you're taking the sabbatical route, proof for you might look like hiring a financial advisor to get clear on (1) how long your financial runway really is, (2) what it really costs for you to live with peace of mind for the foreseeable future, and (3) what it will cost for you to live comfortably later on down the road. One thing you may find is that your cost of living is much lower than the number you've been telling yourself. I'm sharing the financial advisor wisdom with you as something that I would do differently if I had to do this all over again. Money wasn't a sticking point for me prior to either leap. I had ample savings prior to Leap 1, and I had even more at the outset of Leap 2 to the tune of $60,000. To this day, it sounds crazy even to say that out loud, but that was some solid "F-U money," if I have to say so myself.

Even though I had that liquid capital on hand to pay my mortgage and bills for a good stretch of time, I still wish I had consulted with a financial advisor first. About a year after my leap, one of my good girlfriends, Christina, who is a Certified Financial Planner™ (CFP®) and Certified Public Accountant (CPA), shared that she was opening her own financial management firm—Mass Financial Management.

When I got my wits about me, I reached out to enlist her services to get an expert set of eyes on my finances. That $60K in savings wasn't all that I'd managed to afford myself. I'd been proactive while working my way up the career ladder and had taken heed of the financial wisdom imparted by my parents and mentors. But that didn't stop the throes of full-time entrepreneurship from playing tricks on my mind when money appeared to be going out faster than it was coming in. So, I asked for the help that I needed. Christina was able to paint a picture of my financial runway that put my mind at ease. I'd been a little hard on myself and hadn't given myself enough credit for being a great steward of my resources ahead of my leap. Because of my diligence, discipline, and patience, I was able to move forward with even more confidence. I wish that same confidence for you.

Now, if the sabbatical route is not for you and you're planning to roll up your entrepreneurial sleeves and literally get straight to business, proof for you is a bit more involved. In addition to meeting with a financial advisor, proof for you includes packaging, pitching, and profiting from what you have to offer–right now! Here are a few questions to think about and answer to help you hone in on where you need to show up in the marketplace and what "language" you need to speak so that your ideal customer will hear you loud and clear.

What are you planning to do or already selling? Is it a product, service, or combination of both? What's included in your offering? How much does the product or service cost? What's your cost of doing business? How much profit do you want to make from each sale? Who is your ideal client?

I caution you not to settle for *everyone*. Sure, you may allow anyone to buy, but, as a marketer—yes, you—I want you to avoid the rookie mistake of not having an ideal client defined. *Do they already know that they want or need what you're selling?* If not, you're going to have an uphill experience educating them on their problem and the solution you provide before it becomes a desired, viable remedy that they are ready to pay for. It can be done, but make sure you factor in some grace and extra runway for the time it will take. I can laugh about it now, but I definitely took the scenic route.

How does your ideal client talk about the problem that your offer solves? Is your target audience already paying for solutions to this problem? If so, what are those solutions, and why aren't they enough? Why does your ideal client not already have this problem solved? Why do they need your product or service? If they don't need it, then why should they want it?

What's different about what you sell if there are others selling the same product or service? Why should they spend their money with you? Where do they take up space in their everyday life online and offline? If you're planning to market to them digitally, which platform will you focus on leveraging first?

There's all of that and plenty more to think about and plan for to set you up for either success or to fail fast. Just in case you've been misinformed about the world of entrepreneurship, I want you to hear it here. There is a lot of failing that happens, and it's par for the course. How you manage those moments will determine just how far on this journey of freedom and independence you will ultimately go.

You're creating something out of nothing. You must go into it expecting to learn, try, grow, win, lose, succeed, fail, and cry. You can also expect to daydream about updating your resumé and going back to the 9 to 5. When that happens, snap out of it and get back to the drawing board if this is what you really want. And by all means, do it with grace, resilience, honesty, and persistence. If you go into it with your eyes wide open, you'll be better able to brace for impact and weather the wilderness seasons. So, go ahead and work out some of those kinks *now*. Get clear about *what* you do or offer. Get clear about *who* your product or service is for. Then, start talking about it publicly in the spaces where your ideal client or customer spends time. Educate them, give value, speak to their frustrations, and invite them to take the next step to indulge in your offering as a reprieve (i.e., sell something). Unless you've been working in sales and are familiar with not getting paid if you don't sell, then what you're embarking on as a founder and CEO is night and day from the traditional 9 to 5. The success and ensuing financial and time freedom that you're really after is going to require a different level of work and commitment. This pursuit is personal, and it's going to take every ounce of effort and belief you have in yourself.

Being at the helm of your own business is going to require a different skillset that requires you to get out here and market and pitch your business formally and informally. You have to let people know, in essence, that "Hey, I'm here. This is what I'm doing. This is who I'm doing it for, and if that is you, here's how you can get it." That's an oversimplified way of getting at what it will take for you to get either proof that your angle is lucrative or data about what you need to tweak.

Can you answer the questions above? Can you incorporate those answers into content or advertisements that you can share with your existing network with clear instructions on how interested parties can take the next step to buy from you on the spot? If so, you're on your way to generating revenue in your new venture, positioning yourself to create a profit, and, ultimately, relishing in the *proof* that you're onto something.

Proof for me came in the form of former colleagues reaching out for help and hiring me as their coach after seeing my content on LinkedIn, Facebook, and Instagram. Proof came in the form of invites to speak on other creators' platforms and even an invite to share my insights on the local news. Proof came after hosting a seven-day livestream series on "Reasons Why You Haven't Quit." At the end of each livestream, I made a clear and consistent call to action to book a free call with me. That resulted in three calls being booked by prospects who fit the bill of my ideal client. None of those calls converted on the spot, but months later, one of those leads reached out and ultimately became one of my most notable client success stories. More proof. I was on to something.

Proof also came in the form of a reward for on-point *posture*. I had a conversation with two people on my Personal Board of Directors when the business was just a couple months old. I was telling them about my coaching offer and how much the investment was at the time. I offered the option of single coaching sessions or buying three sessions and getting one free. It was something like that. Nevertheless, I shared my pricing structure with them, and they both immediately had reservations about my prices and people's willingness and ability to pay. Without hesitation, I respectfully shut down that rhetoric. I stoically refuted their rationale and emphasized that people have money, and the price is the price. A couple of days later, I onboarded two new clients with ease, and I one thousand percent attribute it to my *posture*. I was both unmoved and certain about the decision I had made about my offer, and the reward soon followed. The funny thing about it is the investment to work with me now is at least five times what it was then, and I've had new clients pay me in full. How's that for proof and a confidence boost?

All of my proof came after I left my 9 to 5, but yours doesn't have to. I recommend getting as much traction as possible *before* you leap. It will increase your confidence and solidify your decision to pivot.

2

Pivot

"You're walking away from a really good job." That was the unsolicited feedback from a coworker when I shared the news about Leap 2. My quizzically sarcastic response was, "*Am I?*" In Chapter 7, I shared that people are going to project their opinions on you about your audacious defiance of the status quo. This wasn't my first rodeo when it came to looking the certainty of six-figures in the face and unapologetically betting on me and God. So, I was ready for it. To the conditioned eye, my decision was completely asinine, but I was determined to trust my gut anyway.

Once you've followed my blueprint, taking the time to pause, reflect on your purpose, devise a plan, put people on notice, assess your posture, and generate proof of concept–there's nothing left to do but pivot. I've used the term *leap* quite a bit throughout the book, but the reality is that quitting your 9 to 5 as a seasoned career professional is actually more of a pivot than a leap. Why? Because when you pivot—at least in the basketball sense—you keep one foot planted while the other foot moves about freely, opening you up to new possibilities, new outlets, and new views that you otherwise wouldn't be afforded if you kept both feet planted.

Before your analytical mind takes off with that analogy, I want to make sure you understand what that planted foot really means. It's not necessarily planted where you are physically. It's figuratively planted everywhere you've been. It's grounded in the skills, experience, and expertise that you've amassed throughout your career. You never lose that. You may allow a few skills to collect dust, but your toolkit is yours to pull from until you decide otherwise, and it's with you everywhere you go.

I had an epiphany sometime after Leap 2 that although my coaching business was new, I wasn't new to business or entrepreneurship. I had all types of relevant experience, ranging from administration and organization to leading projects and people to marketing and photography. I stepped into the ring of my coaching business *in* purpose, but because I felt like I was starting from scratch, I didn't immediately show up as powerful and confident as my credentials afforded me the ability to. I'd forgotten *who* I was for a while, but it was inevitable that I got my swagger back.

There's a sermon that Bishop T. D. Jakes preached some years ago titled "I Didn't Know I Was Me." I mean, he could've ended the sermon right there because the title alone is enough to charge the battery in your back. He reflects on some things that he could have, would have, and maybe should have done if, back in the day, he *knew* who he was. It's no different for me and very likely the same for you. There's not a thing we can do about the past but reflect briefly and glean the lessons. But now that you know without a doubt that you are YOU–i.e., "THAT girl" or "THAT guy"–what are you going to do?

Before you pivot, I invite you to do the following:

1. Pick a date that you want to be your last day on the job. It doesn't matter how far out it is. Why? You guessed it. Because *you get to choose.* Don't judge it or overthink it. Pick a date that's meaningful to you, and then circle or highlight that date on a printed calendar that you already use. No notes are necessary. Consider the circled date a silent declaration and note to self. However you choose to earmark the date, it will simply serve as a subtle—or not-so-subtle—reminder of what's to come.

2. Draft your resignation letter. It's coming regardless, right? I've taken the guesswork out of it and provided a template for you at the end of this book. You have bigger fish to fry, so use my template, date it, and save it for when the time is right. Tweak it if you need to, but the heavy lifting is already done for you.

3. Proactively ask for and enlist the help that you need. Whether it's a therapist, life coach, financial advisor, resources, or all of the above. Ask for what you need and invest the time and/or money required.

4. Pause. Well, plan for it, anyway. The *pause* isn't a one-time occurrence to kickstart your clarity journey. It's a life hack that will serve you until the end of time if you take heed to it.

After putting Leap 1 in motion and then getting recruited back, I took a month of annual leave before starting my new position. I'm almost ashamed to admit that even with taking off an entire month, I still had plenty of leave left in the bank. Prior to Leap 2, I had plans to take my version of an "Eat, Pray, Love" trip to Bali. This time, I'd given a month's notice when I submitted my resignation, and that time frame factored in my two-week vacation, which was already on the books.

After Leap 2 was behind me, I had a little over 20 days until my 35th birthday. My birthday is a big deal, and I don't wait to be celebrated. Anything outside of what I do for myself is extra. So, to take things up a notch, I gifted myself something that I've never had before—the entire summer off. Three months of no work. The gift to just *be*. I had the financial means and lifestyle independence to do it, so that's exactly what I did. It was The Perfect Pattern Interrupt and reset for the full-time entrepreneurship journey that was ahead of me.

One of my clients, Alex, found me when she'd just about had it with her 9 to 5. She's a mom of two, a CPA, and a Financial Strategist. At the time that we met, she'd been serving in the public accounting space doing taxes for about a decade. She was making six-figures, but she was burned out, overwhelmed, and looking for the nearest opportunity to pivot into a business of her own. She wanted to help high-achieving women create their financial exit strategies and also help other entrepreneurs proactively tax plan.

In our case study interview, Alex shared that a couple months before we officially met, she had already dated, printed, and signed her resignation letter, but she couldn't bring herself to turn it in. She enlisted my help to overcome the fear she was experiencing and gain the confidence to give her official notice. In the interview, I probed a bit about the fear because I knew she wasn't alone. Alex shared that a big part of her fear was letting down the people that she'd worked with for so many years. That good ol' loyalty never misses an opportunity to keep you playing small and prolonging what, in your gut, you know is necessary. Unreasonable loyalty is one of those silent killers that keeps my fellow go-getters in places that are no longer serving them at the expense of the sanity and the freedom that their souls desire.

My very first call with Alex was a complimentary Strategy Session. I invited her to work with me to help break away the figurative cement around her feet that was keeping her stuck in a place where she no longer desired to be. Her 'yes' was immediate, and we took the first steps to get the ball rolling and officially onboard her. The very next day, she reached out and said that she'd decided to submit her resignation letter. She'd been holding on to it for months, but after a 30-minute call with me, she'd found the spark that she'd been missing. You'll have to check out her full case study interview on my Danielle The Coach® YouTube channel to hear how her full-blown breakthrough was almost sabotaged and how we managed to avert that crisis. Without giving too much away, I'll share that in less than 90 days of working together,

Alex gracefully bid farewell to her 9 to 5 and fulfilled her dream of pivoting into full-time entrepreneurship.

One of the things that Alex will tell you that I offered her was preparation for life after the pivot. It's the promised land that you long for, but what actually happens when you get there? I knew she was ready to dive into building out her grand vision for her business, but I offered a gentle suggestion to factor in some downtime before hitting the ground running because I knew what was ahead for her.

I cannot stress enough how important it is to *pause* not only before but also *after* you pivot. I get it. We can be so anxious about moving on and finally having the opportunity to work on our passion that we don't realize how important a reset is when preparing to play the long game of entrepreneurship. So again, I offer the same advice to you so you can have the stamina required for the journey that awaits you.

Whether you've been reading this book straight through or taking iterative action that aligns with my blueprint, there's a lot to think and work through to transition out of your 9 to 5 without regret. The 7 P's may end with the Pivot, but know that it's the catalyst to a brand-new beginning and all that's in store for you on the other side of faith and courage. Whenever your day comes, don't pivot lackadaisically. Pivot like the business and life of your wildest dreams depend on it. Pivot like a Six-Figure Quitter!

10

Final Thoughts

"When I found I had crossed that line, I looked at my hands to see if I was the same person. There was such a glory over everything; the sun came like gold through trees, and over the fields, and I felt like I was in Heaven."
-Harriet Tubman

About four years after I left the FBI, I received an invitation to be a virtual guest speaker at a FAAM monthly meeting. The invitation triggered a myriad of feelings. I was mostly elated to know that the group was still thriving years beyond my departure. I felt honored to be invited back and acknowledged as the founder. I also felt a bit of nostalgia sharing space again with some of my closest colleagues who were there when FAAM was just a thought. They'd shown up at that first informal roundtable meeting of the minds. They'd given buy-in to keep the conversation going. They showed up for our leadership development and networking meetings month after month and then year after year. They supported my vision with their time and genius at a time when it was unprecedented, unpopular, and, quite frankly, a risk to their career progression. They graciously and courageously accepted the task of carrying the charge when it was time for the leadership baton to be passed. Most of all, they trusted me and my leadership. For that, I am forever grateful.

My response to the invitation was an emphatic "Yes! I'd love to." My virtual appearance was set up as a Q&A, during which I was interviewed by one of my dear friends who was at that very first roundtable meeting. Let's call him "Jay"—my brother from another. What a lot of people learned that day is that our connection began a decade before FAAM was birthed. We first crossed paths during our time as FBI Honors Interns and went on to land permanent positions as full-time analysts. From HBCU grads to incognito FBI employees, it's safe to say that we grew up in the Bureau together. We were household names to each other's families and celebrated each other's milestones along the way.

That said, the Q&A session was nothing short of refreshing, motivating, and inspiring. Over one hundred FAAM members and allies joined the call, and the chat feed moved what seemed like one hundred miles per second. Former mentors, mentees, peers, and colleagues—some whom I hadn't seen or interacted with since I left—were tuned in, and the love and support were palpable. As only Jay could do, he took me back down memory lane with questions that jarred memories spanning from my summer internship experience to peeling back layers on what led me–the founder of FAAM–to leave the FBI and take the leap.

I was honest, transparent, and tactfully vulnerable about my experience and the fact that, like the birthing of FAAM, my purpose isn't about me. I was just the surrogate in the right place at the right time with the right access and just enough audacity and courage to bring it to life. FAAM served me and made my heart sing in a way that it never had before. But it was so much bigger than me. The proof of that is evident. FAAM is a household name. Who would have thought?!

If there is one thing I learned from my last gig at the Bureau, it's that there is a spectrum for acceptance when introducing something new–be it technical or not. You have your early adopters–those who are onboard with minimal convincing because they either understand the vision or simply trust you as the conduit to success. Then, you have your middle-of-the-way adopters who need to see a little motion or proof before they buy into the idea, concept, or movement. Then, you have your late adopters. They are risk averse and need proof, time, and then a little bit more proof of concept before even considering getting on board. That right there was probably the lesson I was supposed to take away from that last stint because I've experienced people in all three categories when it came to both Leap 1 and Leap 2.

There were the less than a handful of early adopters who immediately supported my decision to take the leap and offered resources and encouragement. There were those middle-of-the-way supporters who were uneasy about my decisions at the outset but whose faith was strengthened when they saw that my faith parachute actually worked. And, of course, there were many late adopters who, initially, were annoyed at my gumption and couldn't fathom me walking away from a "good government job" my way and on my terms. Believe it or not, I can name at least two late adopters who, themselves, have since done the very thing they scoffed at when I did it. They've unapologetically quit well-paying jobs and lived to tell about it. When I think of them, I not only think about that spectrum of acceptance for innovation, but I also think of something I shared with FAAM during my Q&A.

I don't know what Jay asked me, but I'll never forget responding with "Trailblazers blaze trails." It sounds simple until you're the one out front with your tool of choice leading yourself, creating figurative paths and roads to the freedom your soul desires by faith and sheer will. It's hard. It's lonely. It's scary to go first and do something you've never seen anyone or not many other people do. But that's what trailblazers do. Then, one day, they look up and realize they've left not only a trail but a blueprint for others to do the same.

I pray that this book stirred something in you and inspired you to look at yourself and what's possible through a different lens. It is my hope that you recognize just how possible a different life and a different outcome are for you beyond the box of the status quo. It is my charge that you lean into the 7 P's:

Pause to regroup, gather your composure, and center yourself before you do anything else. Disconnect by any means necessary (safely, of course), and then reconnect with a full energy tank and clarity about what's next.

Make your next move *in **Purpose***. You are on this earth for a reason, and your *why* absolutely matters. Your next purpose assignment is calling, so wrap that comfort zone complacency up and lean into that nudge that just won't go away. Even if it scares you.

While you're at it, remember to pack your parachute, aka your *Plan*. How much more confident and likely are you to take a leap if you have a working parachute in tow? Knowing where you're going and having some semblance of how you're going to get there—before you quit—is imperative.

Once you're clear about the direction you're heading and you have a solid plan in place, go ahead and *Put People on Notice.* If for no other reason, do it to control the narrative. You can say as much or as little as your heart desires, but let it be known and say it with your chest. Start with your Personal Board of Directors and then share what's necessary when necessary as you rebrand yourself. You'll be surprised to find out who's already in place to help make your vision a reality and usher you into the life of your wildest dreams. Your networks have never been more vital.

Speaking of saying it with your chest, your **Posture** absolutely matters. How you talk about what you're planning matters (whether it's the next step or the big vision). Your body language and even how you respond to other people's opinions also matter. Your game face is required. Don't leave home without it.

Prove It to yourself, first and foremost, that your venture is viable. Proof of concept will not only increase your confidence but also validate that there is an audience that is interested in what you plan to offer. It will also give you data on whether they'll buy it at the price point that you have in mind.

Last but not least, when it's time—*Pivot*. And pivot like your life depends on it. Keep one foot planted in your skills, abilities, gifts, and expertise and the other foot free to explore life, career, business, and opportunity from a completely new vantage point.

Remember, trailblazers blaze trails. It's not always easy, but it can be done without regret if you give yourself the grace to move through the "7 P's." You making it this far in this book speaks volumes about what you're willing to invest in yourself when it comes to your most valued commodity, your time. This will undoubtedly be one of many investments you will make to bring the vision you've been given about what's next to life. Yes, it can be hard to leave what's familiar, and it can be even harder to leave who is familiar. No matter how hard, I encourage you to always do three things. Choose *courage*. Choose *purpose*. And most of all, choose YOU.

11

Free Gift

I shared in an earlier chapter that I take my birthday seriously. It's currently just after midnight on my 40th birthday *and* two and a half years after I first started writing this book. Although this is not how I ever envisioned bringing in a new decade, I'm setting the stage for what's to come by finishing what I started by any means necessary *and* spreading a little love.

That said, I really appreciate you taking the time to read this book. It was a labor of love to write, and it took brute willpower to birth. I know that this, too, is one of my many purpose assignments, as it has weighed on my conscience for years. I am beyond delighted to finally share my insights and lessons learned with you in this format. It's my prayer that the heartfelt words and stories I shared are, to you, what I wish I had when I was at my wit's end trying to figure out how to free myself from my 9 to 5 without regret.

I have a few free resources that I'd like to share with you to help you take the guesswork out of what's next and also help you pivot like a confident Six-Figure Quitter.

You can access them at
www.thesixfigurequitter.com/resources.